Calmed Earth

Luminous *Harmony*

Lessening Earthquake, Firestorm

Richard Shargel

Summit Sunrise College

www.summitsunrise.org

Education Humanity Foundation

Contents

Luminous Harmony – Lessening Earthquake,   5
    Firestorm, Tsunami

Perfected Peace and Harmony – Attaining God's   22
    Kingdom of Heaven on Earth, the Golden Age

Earth's Response   37

The Seven Spirits, Life, Environment   45

Nature's Solar Life-Fire   51

Environmental Service, Now and Ahead   54

Upheavals Diminished – Perfected Humans and Earth   62

Universal Polarity – Human Empowerment   71

References   80

We are extremely grateful to Editions-Prosveta for the published lectures of the master initiate teacher, Omraam Mikhael Aivanhov, and thank them for the use of brief quotations. Editions-Proseta is headquartered in Frejus, France. The books are available through 28 Prosveta distributors, globally. **www.prosveta.com**.

Thanks also to Laurie David's contributions to humanity's environmental harmony, recorded in her 'The Solution is You! – An Activist's Guide'.

Luminous Harmony

Lessening Earthquake, Firestorm, Tsunami

Today there are two major things helping our environment; one is widely known, the second enormously powerful, yet little known.

Saving forests and planting trees helps absorb air's carbon dioxide and reduce global warming. Nations' reducing industrial gas-emissions helps. Even a person who, at a long traffic light turns off their engine, helps.

Other efforts, as you know, are building dikes at river edges to lesson flooding, strengthening building and bridge foundations, etc. Yet the biggest help is what people themselves are doing, what we as individuals sometimes do.

The full story of how we help reduce environmental upheaval like hurricane, tsunami and earthquake is given us by this recent century's two leading visionaries, master initiates Geoffrey Hodson and Omraam Mikhael Aivanhov. Many people who read or hear it understand with a smile. It's really something remarkable, and reflects what directly helps bring our coming golden age of environmental harmony, happy peace and marvelous perfection.

Humans have a sixth sense, as you know; for example, silently hearing what a friend is about to say. Well, there's a seventh sense we're developing also. The seventh is a direct apprehending/sensing of what comes from above: reality's understanding, initiatic wisdom, truth. Recently, at about 4:30AM I was lightly awake and sensed something superb.

My inner voice said, "Richard, get up and write it." What was heard from above was the first chapter in my book 'Manifesting Spiritual Gold with God's Light'. Later I realized how this gift came.

The top master initiate teacher Omraam Mikhael Aivanhov told us that after his transition he would then be here helping everyone. Not an ascended master, a master *present*, still channeling nature's principles, light and wisdom from above to us worldwide.

Aren't nature's gifts marvelous?

Someday we all will have this seventh sense active, which directly helps create global harmony among humans, a major factor in environmental calmness. Here's how it works for us and for earth and all.

For tens of millennia the energy of our negative feelings and actions, like anger and war, has been absorbed by the earth. And therein is the answer. With kindness, generosity, love, light and helpful activity to one another and the world we help bring back the calm environment. During humanity's first era, before Atlantis, in the era of Lemuria, there was perfect world harmony. The Lemurians were wholly loving, a perfected world family; however they were attacked by the Atlanteans and had to escape down into the earth where they still are! They are 6 ½ to 9 feet tall, never had, like us, a dark age, and have a library miles long with books detailing the world's entire history. I met one of them three years ago; as have other people too.

A Danish sea captain about 150 years ago sailed his boat to the North Pole and descended near to the Lemurian region. Most people do not return, but he did and wrote about it. Well, here is our solution to environmental calmness in the world; what the Lemurians do; what we all occasionally do: **beam love and light to earth**, with the essence of our lives, thoughts, feelings and actions being **divine love and light**.

There is so infinitely much to becoming loving light that, for example, our ways and means today are given to us in 70 volumes of lectures, so far translated from French. God's divine love and light channels through to us through the spiritual sun. I'll explain this briefly, however it'd be best to go directly to the Aivanhov lectures and read it now. The books come from www.prosveta.com.

Let us reflect on nature's harmony so we see how humanity may attain the same, thus nourishing earth.

Humans in the past learned from fish.

Yes, it is true that big fish eat little fish; a tiger eats small animals. However there is a nice plus to this, which is not true of people being angry, upset or creating chaos. When we eat a fruit, vegetable or piece of chicken the soul-energy (one way to say it) of that piece of chicken is advanced by being in a human. The same for sea plants eaten by fish; the plants' spirit-being become more evolved. That's simply how nature evolves all beings.

When the beef-steer is killed for its meat it becomes quite upset. That negative energy is retained in the meat and disaffects the eater. However too, the bit of meat molecules become now furthered within the human. You, everyone, are so vitally important to learn and vitally grow, perfecting earth and all. Aivanhov and Hodson shared most exceedingly valuable truths, beginning with this fact.

The earth's upheavals, like earthquakes, are a result of peoples' millennia of negative action, thought and feeling; and likewise, activity of light and love help assuage such disasters, being directly, **subtly contributive to nature.** The earth absorbs energies of man's war and anger, even selfishness, responding "Get it all together in perfected harmony again like you did first, originally, in the era of Lemuria." One part of 'getting it together' is illustrated by today's science.

There's a lot of creativity in science. Medicine, computers, etc. however science is primarily analysis. Science's main interest is analyzing; in biology, the classification of nearly every animal, plant and mineral; in chemistry, analysis of mixtures, even compounds; in medicine, analysis of health issues. This all involves taking apart, to see, classify, and know. So very much more important is putting together, synthesis, *creating.* Even in our daily thought we tend to do a lot of analyzing in order to understand; yet it's vitally contributive to create, put together, advance things such as environmental and human harmony in the world. It seems a bit unusual, but by our eating we are creating, both for ourselves and the earth.

One of the obvious things not to 'eat' is tobacco smoke. As a medical chemist working at the University of California Medical Center in San Francisco, I saw a tobacco smoke analysis showing 120 cancer-causing chemicals, from an analyzed 400 tobacco chemicals. Slowly poisoning oneself poisons earth, doesn't it, as we each are a living part of planet earth. And the reverse is nicely true; how giving oneself perfected ingestion, - breathed, eaten or received meditating, – perfectly feeds lovely earth, too. We long ago learned this from fish: the environment and earth are naturally developed by humans' eating.

When food – earth – is eaten, digested and eliminated, its molecules, having been in a human, are a little more advanced, evolved. When returned to earth, the earth and environment are then, to a degree, more evolved. Also, at a higher level we, of course nourish the living environment with our love and light.

O.M. Aivanhov explains to us how to comprehensively apply such light and love within every facet of our growth and being. See his **Spiritual Alchemy,** chapter **Living in Conscious Reciprocity with Nature,** pgs. 57-71.

Both Aivanhov and Hodson are two vastly advanced master initiate teachers. The way to make the world *free* of environment upheaval is briefed below.

Today, the beautiful treasures of God's divine love, light and creative powers are more fully understood. The universal principle of transforming is now better known. Just as the feeling of anger is transformed to power for progress and others' good; just as lust, with earnest elevated learning may be directly transformed to one's inner male-female union, the perfection of our loving luminous thought, feeling, will and activity helps calm the earth, as well as evolutionarily advancng our life. Here are three bits I've selected from thousands in Aivanhov's luminously instructive published lectures. This demonstrates how, as we develop in spiritual understanding and meditative power, we directly help calm the earth.

For example, it is important to quickly grow beyond identifying mainly with body, and identify with our Spirit.

"The body is not the man, it is only his car, his horse, an instrument, a dwelling place. The real man is the Spirit, all powerful, unlimited, omniscient Spirit. When man changes and identifies himself with his Spirit, he will become powerful, illumined, immortal, divine." 1

A transformed society, positively aiding our earth beneath, embodies a harmony of true love. Here's how the sun's light begins to be explained.

"What glorious sunshine today. Wisdom consists in understanding that love is more important than anything else. It is high time that men understood that love is at the heart of everything, and that if they make it the one motive power behind every aspect of their lives, the intense heat of their love will be transformed into dazzling light and their intelligence will be illuminated. Illumination can only come from love." 2

Illumination. Light, like the word 'love', is so beautifully immense that it takes hundreds of experiences and learnings to understand. And next century, we'll even be and know more. Thankfully, as you know, there is lovely immense help from above.

Nature's A-Team

Dwell there beings, closely kin

Whose every gesture, guiding whim

Breathes bounding joy, empowering flame!

Then, on an instant, call our name.

One special morning Mr. Hodson and his wife were meditating in their U.K. Epping Forest cottage garden. Hodson asked an archangel for inspiring words of wisdom. Here is blue archangel Bethelda's concluding message from above.

"Be love, your angel self, that through your beauty, God's splendor may be revealed." 3

One of the keys to being one's angel-self.

"Every day, try to re-establish contact with the divine Source so that it may feed your own source, the one that flows within you."

Another way of saying this is "Link with your inner spring of sunshine." Also, in more common words, be clearly focused and sensitive; allow the Christ-spirit to flow through in your inspiration and service.

"Allow this Source to descend first of all into your heart, through love. Whatever happens, whatever bitterness, disappointments or trials you experience, never stop loving, for it is in loving that your heart purifies itself. Then, allow this Source to descend into your intellect, as light. Thanks to this light, you will avoid obstacles and snares; you will discern which path to follow and will advance with confidence. When the divine Source penetrates your soul, it will cause it to expand to the far reaches of the universe. You will merge into the immensity through love; whatever happens, whatever bitterness, carrying all beings with you.

At last, when you have succeeded in allowing the Source to flow in your heart, your intellect and your soul, it will reunite with the primordial Source, which is your spirit, which is God himself. As a result, you will truly live the divine life, which is all powerful." 4

Now that we are in closer in understanding-unity - our lives mutually contributive - grasping the heart of gaining empowerment to strengthen the environment, I must select for you the most highly complete wisdom bit of all, demonstrating with this five minute meditation – best at sunrise - the most powerfully poetic 'personal sunray' that we tens of thousands of us worldwide are practicing. Say this at sunrise to, as you like: God, Nature, the spiritual sun, Lord, the Tree of Life, all.

"As the sun rises over the world, so may the Sun of truth, freedom, immortality and eternity, rise in my spirit.

As the sun rises above the world, so may the Sun of love and immensity rise in my soul.

As the sun rises above the world, so may the Sun of intelligence, light and wisdom rise in my intellect.

As the sun rises above the world, so may the Sun of gentleness, kindness, joy, happiness and purity rise in my heart.

As this luminous, radiant sun rises over the world, so may the Sun of strength, power, force, dynamic energy and activity rise in my will.

And as this luminous, radiant, living sun rises over the world, so may the Sun of health, vitality and vigor rise in my body.

Amen. So be it, for the kingdom of God and his righteousness.

Amen. So be it, for the glory of God." 5

1. *Man's Two Natures, Human and Divine*, O.M. Aivanhov, pg. 28

2. *The Splendour of Tiphareth: the Yoga of the Sun*, O.M. Aivanhov, ps. 71-72

3. *The Brotherhood of Angels and Men*, Geoffrey Hodson, pgs. 78-80

4. *Daily Meditation, July 17, 2005*, O.M. Aivanhov

5. *The Splendour of Tiphareth: the Yoga of the Sun*, O.M. Aivanhov, pgs. 117-118

Environmental activist Laurie David links with her sunshine within, flowing her inner Source selflessly in loving kindness. This is about Laurie, in her book, 'The Solution Is You!'.

"The secret of her effectiveness comes from a clear ambitious vision, boundless energy, and her strong, strategic mind. Her sense of diplomacy and endearing charm disarm even those inclined by politics or prejudice to dislike her. Her most potent weapon is the persuasiveness and confidence that come from an utterly selfless passion."

The essence of endearing passion?: of course, divine love, life's major key, our purest, big 'airplane' of life and progress for all; our loving, selfless, creative service; shared even to dimmies or antagonists.

So what's nature's principle that we apply when challenged by others' opposition? What's our best focus when challenged, helping earth, everyone and everything?

"In the midst of adversity retain fidelity."

Don't react, take in or even feel 'bad stuff'; be faithful to one's loving purpose and activity, retaining *fidelity*.

And too, we appreciate that service to others feeds, at once, the environment, world, universe above, and oneself ahead.

They Who Hunger Shall Be Satisfied

Ancient Caring's inward urge
awakens unmanifested duty

Hunger's 'ssuaging, earth's
lingering adolescence aging

Seek to gather dear
the comprehending few

Touch they whose upward paths
in consort steady climb

Whose labors love enjoins their
sacred goal attained sublime

Make manifest between those staunch of
forward-thriving heart
thy hand's creative bounty true

And render humbly noble
deed in service e'er anew

Listen! Hear the step of
children yet unborn
the yonder yearn of
feelings yet to be

While thunder rents the
errant past so shamely trod

the green abunding earth
shall tend now all

Our aspirations
rapt upward magnifying God
12-19-86

We need to energize all heat generators and vehicles with sunlight, rather than gas. There are 130 new coal plants being built in the U.S. In China, one new plant goes up each week. The technology for the use of solar light increases each decade. U.S. politics needs to make it a top priority; not petroleum. Cars, trucks, planes and ships vitally need to be solar powered, global warming stopped.

Political anarchy is earth-destructive; global harmonious **synarchy** is perfectly beneficial, both here and above.

Perfected Peace and Loving Harmony – Attaining God's Kingdom of Heaven on Earth, the Golden Age

Let's have a look at Lemuria, for an example, its perfected harmony and advanced evolutionary development, then reflect on the magnificent Tree of Life above.

Our era of Lemuria preceeded Atlantis. The Lemurians lived in loving harmony and kindness to all, with loving unity among themselves. Then the Atlanteans came and started anarchy with the world's first dominant, selfish government. The Atlantean people revolted. Atlantis even attacked Lemuria severely, and the Lemurians escaped. There are at least three openings in the earth's surface to large spaces underneath. The center of the earth is not firey molten rock. Our earth below is partly hollow. One of the entries is way north, as discovered by a Norwegian ship captain. Another entry is in Tibet, with a small one in northern California

Highly unique is their huge library with all history recorded. The lovely Lemurians themselves, having had no historical dark age like us, are beautifully evolved living hundreds of years each life. So how, do you ask, do we emulate their perfected lives?

The answer's simple: just as they, and some of us are doing, study, practice and learn the living universe's natural principles – like the higher nature of polarity - and lovingly relate to the earth, angels, archangels and divinities above, you're your divine love.

All of this is a furthered harmony to the Supreme Being, God, as of course God's presence is in every atom of the universe, every human, animal, plant and stone; and directly in the ten sephiroth of the Tree of Life.

The Tree of Life's regions, divinities and marvelous activity is a little explained below. It's shown for us quite thoroughly in the seventy volumes of Omraam Mikhael Aivanhov's lectures.

We all of course love nature; when in the forest or on a mountain, even when we come outside and say 'The fresh air feels good'. I didn't learn until my mid-years that what we are feeling on a mountain, forest, in the outside air is felt with, yes our skin, but more so with our whole inner self; the air inside a house and outside both have 21 percent oxygen. Air's gases inside and out are chemically identical. The big thing about outside as is that there air is more alive, not 'contained' by roof and walls, and thus largely insulated from invisible living beings. What we feel in the outside air is the presence of nature spirits and angels. The same when we take off our shoes because it feels better. Yes, our feet and body feel different uncovered; It's for both reasons: not feeling enclosed and covered, but even more the subtle sensing of near-and-touching nature spirits and angels. One of the amazing things we learn in the universal wisdom teaching is that an angel can even be partly within one. It is entirely known that we do help angels; they definitely do receive from us, especially the more we are consciously evolved.

And our feelings also, when resonant with the luminous realms above, are joyfully received in the angelic worlds' loving-splendor.

Remember? – feelings are like music; there's more to it than merely physical. Just like we are more than a car: our body. We're body, soul and spirit. And further learning shows us that we have seven bodies: the physical, etheric, emotional, mental, causal (higher mental), buddhic (higher love), and atmic (spiritual).

The same for the living universe. It's greatly beyond physical astronomy; the stars and planets. It's hugely practical for development to work with ourself's seven bodies (there are many more) and likewise, it's enormously great to lovingly give and relate to the ten living regions in the heaven above (with many more up to the region beyond the Tree of Life, the realm of limitless light, God the Absolute).

Relating to the spiritual sun is one path. In the cabbalistic Tree of Life for us, there are sixty two beautifully productive paths. One of the biggest is with Tiphareth, our beautifully nourishing spiritual sun. You'll see, reading the universal wisdom initiatic science teaching: O.M. Aivanhov. One's evolutionary growth, progress and empowerment are magnificently accelerated; joyfully, wonderfully. Let's start where everyone understands and relates some, to Mother Nature's forest, mountains, animals, angels.

The angelic realms are immensely helpful to us and the environment, and we to them. I was extremely thankful and happy to learn that angels and divinities above are helped by humans. Our aid to above is a delightful truth and reality.

Sunrise is the main time to pray and meditate. When the sun's just below the horizon the sky's beautifully bright-colored, radiating divine life nourishes earth and us. The sun is the living channel to us through the Tree of Life, from God above. There's so tremendously much to learn about light; people say "Yes" but know, feel and experience just a tiny bit; it's marvelously wonderful to learn more. It would be well even to put this book down until later, immediately reading an O.M. Aivanhov book of lectures, which explain and demonstrate luminous living and *everything else* in his 49 years of published lectures.

It's also at sunrise that the lovely luminous angels most actively hear, speak, and help us, and we them.

Our Christianity speaks of communion; a marvelous communion happens constantly between our angels, the divinities, the Lord on high, and humans. A big event happened a few years ago, in a period of two weeks when angels of air channeled a message to me from on high, through the spirit of Omraam Mikhael Aivanhov. Since it involved birds, and angels' singing, I call it 'Avian Verse'.

Avian Verse

In the 1960's, as a medical service worker, an inner voice led me to begin a study of the world's philosophies, religions and spiritual truths. I eventually became aware of the teachings related to Jesus' own training among the Essenes, with France a likely source. Although I had read a few of Master Aivanhov's books on nutrition and symbolism, it was when I discovered a gold label inside a cover, inscribed Fraternite Blanche Universelle, that I became nearly overwhelmed with joy at what this meant.

History's entire Universal White Brotherhood of initiates, adepts and sages, by both lineage and fraternity, were seen linked through the work of Masters Peter Deunov (Beinsa Douno) and Omraam Mikhael Aivanhov – a circumstance of supremely profound, divinely creative vitality for humanity and the world's future.

Upon following Master Aivanhov's instruction to the use of silence and harmony, my life began to sing as never before. Here then, after first application of the Master's wisdom, is what happened as a prelude to a series of meditations in my garden.

I live on a hill overlooking San Francisco Bay, with acres of meadow and wetlands in between. The view encompasses two mountains, distant cities, three bridges, and vast reaches of hills and salt-water. One afternoon I stood on the rear deck in a fifty-mile gale in rapt fascination, watching a flock of swallows play in the vigorous cross-gusts. High winds swirled every which way. With superb skill the swallows deftly danced, I sharing their joy right through the final surprise. All of a sudden, from two hundred feet over the meadow, one swallow froze its wings in a blazing fast shallow dive. Image a bird six inches wide from one hundred and fifty yards away on an arrow-straight path hitting forty miles per hour through gale cross- gusts, zipping thirty feet past your head.

Little did I know that Mother Earth's eloquent chorus of meaningful correspondences, so often enacted in our atmosphere, was just beginning.

Upon Omraam Mikhael Aivanhov's encouragement – in *A New Earth* – I decided to begin predawn meditations at the rear of my garden where the view of sunrise upon the entire region is most direct. The third day began magically, becoming a glorious peak experience.

5:45 a.m. early June   A quiet of incredible softness. An awakening of infinite beauty bursting with promise rises through vistas of sea, wetland, meadow and distant cities right before you. There, resting on the hills of the sunrise-to-be, a soft pregnant cloud pillow veiled with color. Just now, all the Earth scintillates with portent. And there to the right, from the Bay shallows, a second avian choreography begins, as a line of eight calling Canadian Geese sweeps below you over the meadow, climbing in a giant three-quarter-mile circle high behind and around, returning silently to their migratory way-station on the water. A circle of flight anointing the sacred orb itself, in a moment to rise, sanctifying in turn, all the Earth whose symbolism in these unfolding events may be heard to say, "You have it well within you. Go for it. Now! God's Word resounds through infinite verse, sung throughout our wealth of human experience from boundless repertoire." The next morning at dawn a third avian ballet, equally wondrous, begins.

A Great Snowy Egret, away from its accustomed flyway, discovers a gentle updraft over the meadow. First it glides a perfect circle a quarter of a mile in front below. Then uphill closer another adjoining circle, and with perfect ease another and another, until it circles high above with you at the center, then behind with two more. Seven overlapping circles, each about one hundred yards wide, all on a perfectly symmetrical, arrow-straight northerly path.

Now the imperative is firmly ingrained, and as well the shape of tasks ahead, directed to start with something that could be begun now, done well and thoroughly. Even so, the next morning before dawn, during my meditation, an old thought surreptitiously pokes its nose up, "With all my faults and shortcomings compared with the magnitude of the work ahead, can I really do this?" Immediately the innate harmony of Sun and Earth sang again.

A Canadian Goose flew straight up the meadow. In five years I had not seen one goose over my meadow. Now there were nine in three days. This fellow, with all the concentration he could muster, flew swiftly straight over my head, house, and vehicle parked in front, as if to convey, "Really. What in heaven's name do you need? Claim the opportunity! It is yours. Cannot you see, in the exquisite harmony all around, that none of what you need to do is difficult? Just keep up the momentum. Don't ever stop. Press joyfully onward. Shed the excess: let the creative energies flow. Let Nature happen. It can be so easy. You humans struggle so much. Which of our bird movements takes undue effort? Be like Swallow, Canadian Goose and Great Snowy Egret. Cultivate the supreme joy of flying high, effortlessly."

Our first step in hearing our beautifully magnificent angel-sisters is learning symbolism, the higher language of symbolic meanings singing one's inspired wisdom from above.

We also hear from above when we dream; so hearing the symbolic meaning of our dreams is a nice, lasting learning. When we dream, we are in our astral body in the higher realm above. The language above, heard symbolically, is poetic music.

Hearing symbolically is a step in gaining our seventh sense: directly hearing important truths and realities, such as principles of the natural living universe on high, which powerfully aid humans and all. Hermes Trismegistus did this beautifully 6,400 years ago; as did Rama, Jesus, Buddha, Plato and recently Geoffrey Hodson and Mikhael Aivanhov. Here is the poetic music from above given us by blue aarchangel Bethelda.

Joy   Lovely blue archangel Bethelda sings, beautifully showing us: "You make pictures every time you think; you make music every time you feel, and these things can shine resplendent and beautiful in your world, the beauty of their music filling our ears."

"I would sing to you of joy, the joy of the Gods as
they revel in the land of joy.
The land of joy is the land of dreams, where
every dream comes true.
Where every thought and answering
thought thrills with joy.
The land of joy is the land of the Gods,
there lives the God in man;
For men are Gods, and the Godly part
dwells in the land of the Gods.

The land of joy is beyond the mind,
through the gates of eternal peace.

Angels share that land with men,
and these are the Gods who sing;
Thrills of gladness fill the air,
by joy we live and breath;
Everything there is full of joy,
like bursting buds of spring;
Throughout all the land is the freshness of morn,
of dew, of bud, of flower.
Lightly the angels pass on their way,
wafted on wings of joy;
Nature wears a perennial smile,
a smile that is ever new;
Laughter rings through the woods and dells,
for the joy of eternal spring."

And here's another rose from her, this
essential life-essence: Maintain **"Love-to-love."**

You understand; everyone is born under-standing love-to-love; how could we not? Every atom of earth and life is born of God's love. But connecting one's love to the love of one who antagonizes, or even to an enemy's love, is not yet fully realized. Isn't it true?; this is what we're here on earth for: to use love and light for our highest ideal; working to bring the golden age, God's kingdom of heaven on earth; the divine love being of top importance.

In the U.S., for example, to connect our loving joy with all the love in the middle-east. Sending over, again, our dance, music, entertainment performers, and receiving theirs. Aiding their people's health and prosperity. Thus solving war and bringing loving harmony; as in a loving family, now in a divine loving world harmony.

Here again is our environmental solution; right? Beaming love and light to the earth and sun; in feeling, meditation, creative activity. Experiencing love in feelings is *singing* with the soul. The angels, archangels and divinities receive happily, returning with enormous gifts. My book 'Being Your Symphony' illustrates how it works and what nicely unfolds. Angels of earth beautifully respond; as do angels of water, air and fire.

A bit how singing one's loving feelings works. Our solar plexis, centered 2 centimeters above the navel, is historically our original brain, developing first before our head-brain. In the solar plexis is stored our sun energy; for example, the inspired understanding of spawning intuitive activity.

Both earth and humans are becoming mini-suns.

Another fact of nature is that the sun's rays are returned to it; vastly more than merely physically, like the moon's light reflection. When we kindly give love and light, that energy, that radiance, returns both to the sun and upwardly beyond. Remember?; 'A child's smile radiates to the most distant star'. So healing earth's environment and humanity means 'go for it, all the way, ever'. Intensively study this century's advanced initiate wisdom.

Above, we mentioned going up into the astral world when we dream. Before going to sleep it's helpful to prepare: get ready as for a sacred pilgrimage, bearing fruit in the near and distant future. Also, we may ask for an angel to lead us to a divine school on high where one learns

We advance all day, 24 hours. During the day we read and practice the universal wisdom initiate science teaching. At night too, we ask to enter the divine school above.

You'll then be prepared for receiving occasional inspirational genius, further enabled work toward God's kingdom of heaven on earth, the golden age.

Earth's Response

It's early to see the coming effects in upheaval reduction by man's collective understanding and humanity's harmony. However we know what the earth effects are. In the San Francisco bay area we have 8½ million people. For years the energy and substance of emotion and feelings, including anger, have melded into the region. Two big fires rampaged Oakland, destroying forest and homes, partly due to negative energies absorbed in earth.

Think of what's happened in man's past dark ages; the violence of dictators' self-interest waring destruction. Doesn't it seem reasonable that with today's tsunamis etc. we're hearing from the earth, and above, "Get it together, you humans. Build world harmony and unity, with love, light and creative kindness." Every decade, every year, more and more people understand.

So having the enormous empowering, magnificently perfecting universal wisdom teaching of history greatly furthered is tremendous and enormously useful. Our neighbors within earth, the Agarthans, nicely understand. They never have had a dark age, evolving 100 per cent ever. The Agarthans have a long library, made of rock, using molecular electronics. They themselves, like we growing taller each century, are all over six and a half feet tall, and are old each life. One man said, "I am 450 years old."

Agarthans are interested in chemistry. A man walked into the Mt. Shasta town market, bought detergent, and paid for it with gold.

I was at a dinner meeting south of Mt. Shasta, and heard someone say, "I lived in Mt. Shasta and remember seeing Agarthans sitting at a cave entrance, looking out. Their lovely divine loving societal maturity helps us people on earth's surface. Occasionally, also, one of them comes to aid us.

This happened with me when I prayed to have my male-female polar empowerment increased. An Agarthan lady visited me twice, the first time in her astral presence, and the second time personally.

Earth's natural response, with lesser upheaval, is interesting. Rocks, stones, and minerals evolve, as do plants, animals and humans. In spirit and too, molecularly, minerals become plants, plants become animals, animals become humans, and we are becoming angels. It's simple in the living universe's life-principles. This is how the spiritual sun helps the world grow. This is partly how our divine Supreme Being above emanates and develops life. Just imagine how it'll be years ahead when, instead of seeing accidents and troubles reported in the news, we see reports of nations' friendship and our collective, generous kindness and happy progress. It'll be awhile before enough lessened earthquake etc. is noticed; meantime we'll have more, for nations globally to get it together and gain harmonious unity. So every thought, feeling and activity of selfless inspiration and kindness is directly helpful.

With the understanding and wisdom from above we are taught how to live in harmony with all the different forces and worlds that exist, so that we no longer need to be torn apart by inner conflict and contradiction. This century's universal wisdom initiate science teaching also reveals how man is constructed and what exchanges his soul and spirit need to make with the forces of nature.

I had earth's response this month bigger than ever. Just like earth receiving more each century from humans, and being a bit more environmentally furthered, I've received hugely more every decade, and even feel 3 1/2 lifetimes furthered.

Seven weeks ago I moved 70 miles. Things worked out some; I realized that I had to move again 40 miles north where I'd lived and worked for two decades. I knew this former home-area well; and in subtly helpful ways it knew me.

Before I began moving I thought, "I wonder, if, like times before, things will beautifully come together." Well, more than ever in my life things happened here, tremendously toward furthering my service to the environment and humanity.

The site for my Summit Sunrise College was found, with people there already working in the college's education service. My new residence was found with four of the best room-mates I've ever had; the house-owner dedicated also to human harmony and world service.

Even my need for a home with view to the east, for sunrise, happened. The sunrise seen outside my window is the most beautiful in America; it includes the clouds over the Berkeley east bay hills, the clouds over the San Francisco Bay, and the fog coming in from the Pacific Ocean through the Golden Gate. This collection of vapors gives enormously intense and varied sunrise coloration. One morning, within an hour and a half, standing near the edge of the bay, I saw the sunrise go through five beautiful phases, from vapors over distant hills, the San Francisco Bay, and the Golden Gate ocean inlet.

Two days ago I met a woman better prepared in the acceptance of Summit Sunrise College's learning than anyone in the recent three years. And yesterday the best-prepared, most go-for-it, actively serving student ever, found me!

Nothing, of course, happens by accident. The reality of 'things coming together' is the natural law of corresponding-events, one of the many universal principles that we learn. What in nature is directly involved?

Well, even our children read about it: stories about fairies. When my daughter was very young, and about to live near a forest, she asked, "Are there really fairies in the woods?" Hearing, "Yes",

I'm sure she experienced the subtly living unseen beings in the forest. In the 1920's there were books published with photographs of angels and fairies that children were seeing. Today many people sense, even hear what angels say to us. So what's the message?

Study, learn and meditate more and more with nature's universal Tree of Life here, above and within.

And as dear archangel Bethelda says, "Build bridges to the angelic realms." As all top initiate masters, directly and broadly guide your meditation into the 62 paths of the cabbalistic Tree of Life with its ten sephiroth; the central pillar, earth, moon, sun, to the region of limitless light, God the Absolute in the Ain Soph.

Our Cabbalistic Tree of Life

And as well, of course, environmentally, we do all to reduce toxic emissions.

At schools, parents are often lined up in carpools from five to twenty minutes. Crossroads School in Los Angeles posted a no-idle sign in its carpool lane, which made a nice difference

Many people are biking to work and around; another direct aid. No gas emission; instead exercise. Also, we need to plant trees, and use leaf blowers less, which emit gas emissions in an hour equal to a car driven 150 miles.

Random House estimates that by year 2020 its shift to recycled paper will save 550,000 trees, reducing greenhouse gas emissions by 88 million tons and save 425 billion BTUs of energy.

Germany has a train using magnetism to keep it up and powered forward. The train is repelled upward off the tracks by a magnetic field, the train moving *silently.* In the future, like gliders, planes will be silent too, powered by light. In 'Toward a Solar Civilization' O.M. Aivahov tells us, "In the future we shall all draw our light and heat from the sun. We shall travel thanks to the sun's energy. We shall even be nourished by the light of the sun."

One year, at sunrise meditation, I felt food being made inside of me. I met a healer-teacher who had a significant amount of food made inside him. However, I instead choose life and spirit nourishment, which constantly comes.

Regarding conservation, using less electricity helps; like lowering air conditioning, using compact fluorescent bulbs, which use two thirds less energy and last a lot longer. Big thick TVs and computer monitors use a huge voltage for casting electrons to light the screen. Thin TVs and monitors operate on very low current and don't emit x-rays contributing to illness. A solar powered house is a nice help, thoroughly worth it. These physical means are commonly understood. Quite powerfully effective too are our subtle means to balance environment harmoniously.

The Seven Spirits, Life, Environment

Let's understand the body's and environment's common inner-nature. Both have the seven rainbow colors as principle life-energy emitters. Both the body energy centers and the rainbow have these seven primary colors: red, orange, yellow, green, blue, indigo, violet, which both absorb and emit energies.

Each color has a powerful activity. Fourteen colors are used to cure 331 diseases and conditions. Absorbing *earth's light* of rainbow colors is used in energizing and healing, too. Many healers use earth's luminous energy to powerfully aid healing.

Understanding and using the rainbow colors helps accelerate empowerment, perfection and faster life-evolving; and of course is another step in – if hundreds of millions of us did it - calming our environment.

Appreciating at sunrise the colors in the sky helps. Saying to the living spiritual sun, "Beloved dear sun, may my aura be as empowered as yours." Knowing that sunrise solar radiance and sky/vapor colors is another speaking to humanity from above; in the lovely music of heavenly color, light and movement.

We can also tell which body energy centers need balancing and coordinating. We douse body chakras with a pendant. This tells ones need improving. Then we draw that color up from earth, absorbed with breathing inward.

Then too, appreciating the seven primary colors when we see one in a flower always feels good. When he was a boy, the master teacher O.M. Aivanhov painted one by one the rainbow colors on his window, to see the effect of that colored light shining through. The seven primary colors are colors of the spirits of life – red, the Spirit of life; orange, the Spirit of holiness; yellow, the Spirit of wisdom; green, the Spirit of eternity; blue, the Spirit of truth; indigo, the Spirit of force; and violet, the Spirit of sacrifice.

We are to use the colors to advance. It is good to work with white light; white combines and unites all the colors. White light can give you the omnipotence of purple; the peace and truth of blue; the wealth and eternal youth of green; the wisdom and knowledge of yellow; the health, vigor and vitality of orange; and the activity and dynamic energy of red.

A lady in Europe played symphonic music to patients in the specific key - C to B – that they needed for healing. Even wearing clothing in that vibrational color helps.

In music, the seven colors have their corresponding notes in the musical scale, red C, orange D, yellow E, green F, blue G, indigo A, violet B. The frequency of the note A is 440 vibrations per second. 440 waves per second is in the middle C octave.

One octave below middle C nature makes molecules of that corresponding molecular weight in our body. A healer-friend from Los Angeles had an illness. Meditating one day, a brilliant entity above told him to sound a precise frequency with a low frequency speaker. The man made that exact frequency sound, producing penicillin in his body which cured the illness. (He was allergic to penicillin; the sound-made penicillin caused no allergic reaction).

A lady from Ohio taught the use of low frequency sound for healing. One day she and a friend were walking in the forest. Ahead of them she saw a cylinder tube on the ground. She picked it up. Immediately she was connected to a UFO in the sky, which gave her a special physical ability: to hear the sound frequency missing in a person's voice, and to sing that exact frequency to him. A few days later her daughter fell from her back-yard swing, badly hurting her leg. On the way to the hospital, her mother followed in her car, singing the note her daughter needed. In the hospital's emergency room the doctors were surprised to see that the girl's bleeding had stopped.

Months afterward, while the lady was touring the country healing and teaching, she met a man who had a bad snake-bite. She voiced his needed note and healed him.

The use of colors is healing, too. The method used in India, and a Pennsylvania hospital, shines a specific color of light on a person. 331 illnesses are alleviated. A young girl was severely burnt when her clothing caught on fire. A lady doctor saw her the next day and shined the needed light colors on the girl's body. Seven months later the girl's skin was more velvety perfect than before.

Also powerfully effective is when a healer uses earth light, through the healer into the patient.

And very universally powerful is one's use of spiritual solar light, the hundreds of empowering details explained in the 70 books of Aivanhov lectures. Perfected health, and much else, is attained for the rest of one's life and lifetimes ahead.

Here's one of nature's principles, as is channeled to us.

"When human beings understand that their work starts with themselves, when they begin to change their body and their brain, everything else will change too. Then the earth will truly be the receptacle of Heaven.

How can we transform the earth? By eating it. This is another thing that science has never really understood: why we eat. We eat earth. Oh, of course, it doesn't look like earth because it is in the form of fruits and vegetables, but it is still earth, and it has to go through us and be swallowed, digested and eliminated, over and over again until it is imbued with the emanations and vibrations of our thoughts and feelings. Once the earth is thoroughly impregnated in this way it will have become so subtle that it will be the Kingdom of God. One day the earth will be luminous and transparent because, as it goes through us, it gives us something of itself but it also receives something from us, something of our thoughts and our feelings, something of our vitality; already the earth is not the same as it was in the remote past. It has evolved a great deal and is much subtler and more intelligent because all the human beings who have ever lived on the planet have worked to change it."

We learn from the highest initiate masters like Rama, Jesus, Buddha, Plato, Hodson, Aivanhov because strictly speaking there's one single powerfully beautiful luminous loving path. Yes, everyone too is doing little pieces of it, yet it's true: there's one cosmos, one Supreme Being, one emanation of God from the region of limitless light.

Nature's Solar Life-Fire

Fire burns. Negative thoughts and feelings transform and thus 'burn'. Sun and earth give us the message, "Clearly nourish yourself with a perfected purity of feelings and thoughts." Every feeling of joy, each thought of loving-service, smile and serving-act puts out positive energy to the earth and unseen beings, helping reduce fire and upheavals.

Gradually, with a study of the teaching and undistracted clear focus, we have, rather than noise-making, more constant singing, mentally and emotionally. When I think of a harm, even remembering something of the past, it makes noise, compared to a thought about something good for now or tomorrow. The feeling and thought of the good thing makes *music*.

This is why sideways thoughts, like "That car jumped ahead of the one to its side," "I again remember mistaking your name," feel uncomfortable. Thinking "I'll phone my son," or "Let's have a party to help students in need," - those ideas make 'music', singing above.

And blue angel Bethelda tells us to guide our thoughts and feelings to be harmonious music; oneself even becoming a divine loving 'symphony'. As you know, the work inside that we do is developmentally superb for us.

Transforming violence to gentle loving kindness aids earth's 'music', even in little things. I was asked to use purer detergent for washing clothes. There's less forceful bubbling; and less rinsing needed to get out strong chemicals. That means there's even a bit less negative energy seeping into earth. Also, with the music we hear, when music is sung, or played with violin, it's pure and luminous. The electronic ring of a telephone is less pure in vibration to us and earth. Popular music's drum beat is mainly noise. Percussion should be eliminated at once, in music, thought and feeling, and of course in politics. Nations are to become more friendly, for a thriving world-family. A powerful illustration is in marriage.

When one understands and progresses the inner male-female union, then kindness, love and compassion for people help get blessings for them. This represents the triangle of the spirit pointing down, towards humanity.

God to us
hugely

We to God
a little

Then one receives a ray of divine light from God, and light beams from him in seven colors all the way through heaven, and all the angels and archangels, even the Almighty, marvel at its beauty.

Thus too, just like a child's smile beams to all, even a distant star, one's divine light in every service rendered helps all and everything, earth and environment. You can visualize how the earth works like this too, receiving divine light and rendering it to all. The earth – people too – are becoming suns. Living light is constantly being returned to the sun, and above. Thus, hundreds of millions of us reaching this higher life level together shall directly diminish the environment's upheavals and bring peace.

Environmental Service Now and Ahead

Laurie David's intense activism, socially, politically and industrially, has led to several environmental gains. Another activist is a Kenya resident, Wangari Maathai, who spent thirty years inspiring the planting of trees across her country, and spreading the message that protecting the environment protects democracy. She was the first environmentalist to win a Nobel prize.

The world's and U.S. civil rights' movements make progress, however political improvement is critically vital, and gradually coming. We had Jimmy Carter for president, and the first thing he did was phone the Russian leader to establish friendship. The ages-old feeling of egocentricity among national leaders is what gets them elected. That's their greatest talent: getting themselves into political leadership. Giving support only to environment-aiding politicians is important. When our coming golden age's politics of divine loving *synarchy* replaces selfish anarchy, then both the environment will be calmer and humanity will have attained its harmonious world unity.

Our Environment Above

Both earth and the human body are models of the living universe above. The earth is a sphere; the earth emanated through the God's divine love and light beaming through the spiritual sun; as did we come too. The whole living universe emanates from the region of limitless light above, God the Absolute. We are, of course both born and nurtured of earth substance, and return that living gift as evolving-aid to the earth when we eat, digest and eliminate, and especially when we give divine loving light to nature and earth.

We are born and nurtured from the living splendor above, returning that love and light with developmental growth and loving service to earth, others, and the angels and divinities above

Today driving slowly in town I was meditating, while seeing beauty and movement all around, and feeling harmony in every tree and being. At a stop sign I shined upward sanctifying light to God. At that very moment a bird with food in its mouth landed on the telephone pole wire right in front of me. I heard it! "By helping to sanctify the lovely beings above, even God, humans too are *fed.*"

That fits with nature's principle, "What you give you also receive." It makes a huge difference if what's given is divine loving light.

Environmental Healing Exercises
a. Radiating Light

This is an exercise in giving to nature and to people, from your good will and power to richly help.

In a park or with trees, shrubs and grass, give love and light to the trees; to mother nature.

Stand on the trees and the ground and give love and light to mother earth. "Oh you lovely earth, you are so splendid. My love and light goes to you." or "Wonderful earth, you are so magnificent. Divine love to you all, dear ones." In your own words.

In a shopping mall or downtown area, focus clearly, looking at people, oneself feeling happy. Beam divine loving light to them.

When you see a person who looks a bit luminous, say hello, then something like "What a magnificent day." Or "That's a neat jacket." If they respond "Thanks," then say something like "This is such a pretty area." or "The children over there are so beautiful." Or "I'm learning that this neat harmony you and I enjoy is helping nature reduce earth upheaval." Say to the people whatever of friendly rapport.

Again, now, getting to the essence. "One of the best known passages in the Gospels is the one in which a scribe asks Jesus: 'Which commandment is the first of all?' and Jesus answers, *'You shall love the Lord your God with all your heart, with all your soul, with all your mind and all your strength'.* With this reply Jesus defines a human being as being made up of four psychic principles: the heart, the soul, the mind (faculty of thought), and the spirit (strength). Once they have grown in intelligence, love and wisdom, the heart and mind will become a son and daughter of God.

b. **Rising to Universal Sun, Divine Spirit**
Visualize a meadow. Then visualize effort-lessly climbing a mountain. Now see yourself on the mountain top, saying a prayer on the mountain top. Visualize giving love and light to the angels.

Meditate; feeling yourself identify with spirit. Give love and light to God.

Play a piece of beautiful music and meditate. A most perfect piece is the 7 minute interlude for two flutes and harp in Hector Berlioz' chorale, L'Enfance du Christ. Get the CD. The chorale is magnificent, powerfully aiding yourself, the environment, earth and angels above. Also, Berlioz' CD Te Deum – the only music titled "To God" - is extremely beautiful and powerfully helpful.

c. Nutrition Hrani Yoga: Recycling Earth Higher

Look what eating does for the person; animals and plants too. We of course are more than this temporary car, the body, and so is earth. To add to the earth's higher being, we give it love and light, and eat, consciously, using nutrition-yoga to feed our upper bodies - causal, buddhic, and atmic. Thus too we are evolving ourself, earth and the environment.

The lecture book 'Hrani Yoga: the Yoga of Nutrition' demonstrates for you in detail.

While eating, to nourish our upper mental body, the causal, we think and feel where this food we are eating comes from. "Oh you corn, you are fed by the soil, water and sunlight. Your yellow is the color of the sun."

Then, rather than focus so much on the food's taste, we give love to the food, feeding our upper love-body, the buddhic.

And we feed our atmic body, spirit, by contemplating these three at once - the God-seed in the food, the God-sprout in oneself, and God Himself. Thus the food is more nourishing to earth and the environment, as we do the hrani meditation and spiritually advance both ourself and earth. The more millions of us doing this, then the more our environment and earth harmoniously perfects.

d. Tree of Life: Introduction

Learn the ascending bodies. Astral, emotional – causal, mental – buddhic, love – atmic, spirit.

In meditation visualize rising upward through them one by one to Universal Spirit, the worlds of angels, archangels and divinities.

Now sense what you want to do in meditation. There are endless opportunities.

Examples: Talk to the trees, telling them they are wonderful and beautiful. Tell them that the Kingdom of God, Heaven on Earth is coming, and to help by they telling the other trees, which they do

Meditate love and light to the Throne of God, way above in the region of the Ain Soph Aur. In the Tree's center, give love to the Sun, region Tiphareth.

Do the breathing exercise for self-purification. Inhale purity. Hold your breath feeling the purity absorb into all cells. Then exhale the purity to family, friends, loved ones.

Etheric Earth

Ether is our fourth state of matter: solid, liquid, gas, ether. There are many other states of more subtle living material, just as we have more than the three; body, soul and spirit. It is superbly useful to work with our seven: physical, emotional (auric), mental, etheric, causal (higher mind), buddhic (love) and atmic (spirit). Our earth too has its physical and etheric being. The etheric body gives nourishment to the physical body, and vice versa.

When viewing earth, realize its lovely etheric being, feeling, giving it one's symphony of love.

Humanity Perfected – Upheavals Diminished

The above, practiced and learned, aid lessening earth's upheavals. When love and light exceed anger and war the earth and environment will begin to come back to the balanced harmony it had in the Lemurian era. We humans will be in closer world family, united socially, politically, and in loving harmony with God's magnificent living worlds above. Most vitally key is to nourish oneself with the universal wisdom initiate science teaching, always, 24 hours a day. For example, advance with from master teacher Aivanhov's lectures channeled from on high.

What's ancient, and said by the six world religions, is like a little steam. What the recent initiate wisdom advancement has for you is an entire living ocean. Here is a quote from the book, 'A New Earth'.

"The earth has the particular property of swallowing up our impurities. It acts as a magnet to attract and absorb every kind of dirt and impurity; and sends it all down to be processed and transformed in its underground laboratories. You can see for yourselves how the earth absorbs and transforms all your wastes and gives them back to us in the form of flowers and succulent fruits. This is why, whenever you feel weighted down by problems, anxieties or impurities, I advise you to give them to earth. Make a little hole in the ground and put your fingers into it, and then talk to the earth as to an intelligent, living being, asking it to relieve you of all that torments you. Say, 'O Earth, my Mother, you have given me all the elements of my physical body and I thank you for them. And now I beg you to take away all the impurities that have been accumulating in me for years, and to send them to your marvelous workshops and laboratories. Transform them into the purest elements and then send them back to me, so that I may accomplish my work in the world."

Yes, just like mother and child, mother-nature, earth and humans are a loving family.

We're learning. The bible says, 'Be as children,' meaning to receive from our parents above; and consciously receiving and giving with mother earth and the environment. And a major part of our environment are the four elements fire, air, water, and earth; each with its archangels and angels. Specially expressive to us are the angels of air. 'Avian Verse' demonstrated our angels of air brilliance for you.

In college, I asked my chemistry department chairman why the sky is blue. He couldn't answer. Science doesn't yet know what in earth's atmosphere filters sunlight leaving just blue in the sky.

However, initiates know why the sky's blue. If your aura has a lot of blue the seventh sense is enhanced, You can distinguish truth in many circumstances.

Remember the color of archangel Bethelda? Blue. The sky's blue, beaming blue realities to earth, endowing heaven's understanding, the power of nature's universal principles of truth to earth's every atom.

Think now why clouds are white. What would white clouds represent, symbolically saying?

Heaven's truth shining into water – clouds – brings all to us; all we need for developmental growth and steady evolving; white – made of every color – for every leaf, squirrel, inspiration and attainment. And what do the white clouds do? They rain and snow. Truth rains to us every second, everywhere, for all we need and aspire to, in environmental and human perfecting.

And as we observed earlier, the sun's rays being reflected back to the sun, then truth's use by people is returned through our spiritual sun to God in divine love, light and service, collectively more and more.

Now, how about what the raindrops do.

Have you noticed how much a dog likes to swim? Don't you feel good in a bath, and swimming? In Japan, for their harvested fruit, they do not rinse it in sprayed water, but rather dip the fruit in water. Why? Remember, we and all have also an etheric body. Sprayed water washes away some of the etheric; dipping enhances it, because then the water energy is wholly absorbed.

When bathing or swimming you are in direct contact with the lovely unseen beings in water: water spirits and angels of water. This is another path above; for example, "Oh beautiful angels and wonders of water, dear archangel of water and divine Mother; love and light to Thee all."

You know that water dissolves salts. Water is broadly receptive. Receptivity is feminine; that's why water is feminine and Mother-Nature - divine Mother above – is directly received when in water.

And we have water in our tissues and blood, right? That's another way the God-seed's within.

In addition to sensing angels, feeling their presence outside and in water, we feel them – earth's beautifully living-radiance – a third way. When you have your shoes off isn't it comfortable? The bottom of the feet on the floor feel a special sensation. Shoes and socks, like clothing, like a house, make insulation - a wall - between ourself, somewhat, and the living world beneath. You can also feel this difference, the vibratory energy of the earth, when you walk from a cement sidewalk to the ground, especially awhile after you've been beaming love and light to beloved earth, the living portrait of God's beauty.

Learning nature's truths, life's universal principles, practicing them, and giving divine love and light to the angels and heaven above is again injesting; this time truth, the living food from above, God's solar spiritual life-wisdom. .

Just like the word 'love', 'spirit' is inexpressively vast; greater than can be said in mere words. Even describing our environment is endless. That one's inner and outer worlds resemble one another make it easier to know, enjoy and use for service to others.

The inner and outer worlds. Inner pentagram is you. The outer is the universe.

Our five initiate virtues: the philosopher's stone: **knowledge and understanding**; the fount of everlasting life: our **eternal living**; the universal panacea: a diamond sphere channeling *light, universal wisdom* coming through; the magic mirror: reflection of the *divine, image of God within*; the magic wand: *ability to create wonders and lasting excellence*.

The five lovely key qualities we work to develop are intelligence, love, beauty, nobility and strength. O.M. Aivanhov's 'Light Is a Living Spirit' lectures explain solar light's gift: "It is light that speaks, sings and creates, and as it gradually clears a passage for itself within the human soul, light is reflected in the form of *intelligence, love, beauty, nobility and strength*."

Stars also speak.. You are a star in each meaning of the word - a light-shiner to others, and star of your growing high and noble ideal, helping create and attain our golden age, the kingdom of heaven on earth - resembling our heaven of joy, divine love, brilliant wisdom, and magnificent perfection.

We pray, meditate, contemplate, and identify. Let's identify, to bring heavenly calm and peace to earth and humanity. Remember, with the yoga of nutrition we, at once, identify with God and the God-seeds in the food and oneself. So, choose what you wish to identify with like, for example, environmental calmness and perfection; and at once, a calm perfection within.

Just as there are several trinities like Father, Mother, Holy Ghost; body, soul, spirit; mind, heart and will; in life here and above there are several fives. Let us identify, contemplating these five in life's luminous advance: **kindness, justice, wisdom, love and truth.**

For a little workshop exercise, write each on a line you feel appropriate.

Philosopher's Stone _____

Eternal Fountain _____

Universal Panacea _____

Magic Mirror _____

Magic Wand _____

then write the five around the above pentagram. And, if you want, do the same with intelligence, love, beauty, nobility and strength.

There's a meditation that works beautifully here. Just about the biggest way to radiate light above, to and through the angels, archangels and divinities; to the Supreme Being.

We hear from blue angel Bethelda, *"Be love, your angel self, that through your beauty God's splendor may be revealed."* Grace is one thing;

even more, is sanctity. We are given grace, and to an extent, some sanctity. What's interesting is that we too can sanctify God, when we see beauty. When you see something beautiful, beam sanctity to God.

Then one may think, "If beauty will sanctify, then what else?" Ah, harmony. Even movement. So when I see trees, clouds, sky, flowers, animals, I think and feel radiant sanctification to God above. Try. It feels so good.

Universal Polarity –
Human Empowerment

Nature's, life's, empowering principle is polarity, a pairing of the two rich high forces Divine Mother and Heavenly Father. We immediately begin to understand, as these forces imbuing every region and being in nature's, the universe's entire Tree of Life, are embodied and nourished by God's polar emanation: Yes. *Heavenly Father and Divine Mother.* More understanding comes when we learn that every feeling, thought and desire toward our *complementary* gender has this rich, inner purpose: to elevate and empower one's inner male-female union.

When we read in the initiate science teaching that this inner male-female union is the a tremendously empowering force and means, it makes sense, feeling precisely right, helping us truly go for it; working toward and realizing a perfected inner male-female union.

Polarity is everywhere in nature and the living universe, beginning with Heavenly Father and

Divine Mother. In the cabbalistic Tree of Life polarity begins with God's loving-light descending through the top sephira, Kether, into the pair, Chokmah and Binah.

A manner of polarity in oneself is feelings, emotions, our astral self which is female, and intellect which is male. When a couple newly married join and develop spiritually before physical intimacy that's what they're doing: developing and perfecting their inner male-female unions, while closely relating to Divine Mother and Heavenly Father, and things in nature which are male and female; like water, female, when they take a bath; and the solar presence, male, when they meditate at sunrise.

Receptiveness, receiving, like water's ability to dissolve salts, is female. The moon receives sunlight and is feminine. Forth-going, giving like the sun, is masculine. Yet too the sun receives, both God's divine love and light to radiate to earth and all, and also a return of light from planets, beings and humans. So the sun's at once both masculine and feminine; in perfected male-female union.

And thus earth, our environment, and ourselves are becoming perfected in this lovely union; with the ways and means explained in detail by the initiate science teaching.

Earth and our environment are importantly affected by both man's positive and negative male-female activity. Achieving an excellent under-standing, practice and attainment of inner male-female union is directly helpful to our planet and environmental freedom from upheaval. One way of saying it is that the fire of destruction transforms into man's fire of lovingly empowered creative brilliance.

We read from a Brazilian doctor that heat is healing. That makes sense. The sun, fire, warmth. When I'm in a sauna, it's really hot, about 135 degrees. About 12 to 20 minutes does it. I love it, and give love and thanks to the archangel of fire.

Then, in the spa – the hot tub - we have both, water and a temperature of 104 degrees.

When its warm outside I'm thankful. When it's raining I'm thankful. If humans originated as little animals from the ocean; the ocean giving life to fish, and if we have lots of water in our body, then isn't it obvious that water is alive? Even the silicon dioxide molecule in a grain of sand has a bit of living energy. Yes, earth is *resonantly alive* and singing, even resembling, as we, God's beauty.

Music comes from way on-high. The angels of a top sephira, Chokmah, sing, "Holy, holy, holy." Man's great symphonies and oratorios were inspired from above.

Beauty, Harmony and Movement

There is a way earth and humans move more than just physically, with the globe/body. When at night we dream, we are above in our astral body. And a few people can travel in their etheric body. I met a lady who does etheric travel when she wants. Talking with her after a church service, she told me how she travels astrally to visit her sister in New Jersey, seeing how she is and what she's doing.

In 2004 I prayed to God that I'd done everything I could to unite my inner male and female; and to please help. Weeks later, I was visited by the etheric body of an Agarthan, seeing her for 1½ hours; then two weeks later she came in her physical body to and nicely help. We were together for ten minutes. She smiled at me. I smiled, channeling all the sunlight I could; then she too smiled with solar light to me. It was magnificent, one of the most evolutionarily accelerating experiences I've ever had.

(Lemuria, below earth's surface, has its own artificial sun).

Earth of course rotates on its axis and revolves around the sun. A few of earth's humans are evolved enough to travel astrally in the solar system; even visiting the sun, and occasionally regions and divine beings in the Tree of Life.

Here's how to reach the realm of God, the Absolute, in the region of everlasting light, above the Tree of Life, where God emanates the whole universe and all life. More than simply endowing grace, this meditation emanates, *sanctifying*.

We have three ways of sanctifying God; when we see beauty, contemplate that beauty sanctifying God. Also when we, at once, see beauty, harmony and movement, contemplating those three, sanctifying God. What more highly serving meditation than to have the immense privilege of sanctifying dear God?

Nurture to Ultimate Eternal Heights

How fabulously superb it is to focus one's study for life-nourishment and service. Another principle appreciated is that what is given is received. What is given to others, to earth, to the luminously lovely living Tree of Life above is received in blessings ahead; in ways to oneself, everyone and everything. To be a 'virtual' marcher means being active, like being a forum participant, in the internet's environment-healing websites and organizations. One good site is www.cleartheair.org . It has science studies, such as "Forced and Unforced Ocean Temperature Changes in Atlantic and Pacific Tropical Cyclogenesis Regions," B.D. Santer, T.M.L. Wigley. September 11, 2006.

Another site is www.godsdivinelove.org.

Internet activity of course is creative. Computers, the internet and forums were created; as products of our inventive inspiration. In recent years, what has your inventive inspiration created?

I went to my son's university athletic celebration. There was a nice parade. The school's band marched and played. When, in front of me, the brass blared – trumpets and trombones – I felt, "I transform this blaring into beautifully lovelyness, beaming it to the angels above."

This meditation is done during noise heard, like leaf-blower or truck. You see how this too helps nature, the environment, the lovely earth spirits and angels? You have the opportunity to create your own energy-aid, like this, to earth and above. Every bit directly helps; our collective aid to earth, each other, the environment and entire living universe above, ***together exponentially helped***: $2^3 = 10,000$. "A child's smile radiates to the most distant star." Your inspired work for others radiates to everyone and the heavens above, nourishing to eternal heights.

It is known by our leading visionaries what magnificence awaits, centuries ahead; what we all are here to help realize and attain. The top-most best? It's clear. Humanity's highest ideal focuses luminously progressive activity ahead: ***realizing the Kingdom of God, heaven on earth, the Golden Age: attaining ultimate joy, divinely loving nobility, luminous harmony, and magnificent perfection.***

Yes. Heaven is not a spot or place; heaven is supreme joy, divinely loving harmony and magnificent perfection. All in nature adds to evolving beauty and perfection; each person serves, helping. Too, we learn and advance from overcoming problems, transforming darkness to blessings, to loving harmony, global unity, joy and light, for oneself, the world, and heavens above.

Divine love - loving oneself within, one's loving solar-spring radiating service to others, angels above and the Supreme Being. At minimum, world peace is attained and held; loving-brotherhood, global unity, earth's family becoming a unity of splendorous harmony.

Earth's calming environment and humanity's luminous harmony emerges as described in "The Splendour of Tiphareth" of Omraam Mikhael Aivanhov. Our clear understanding is nicely key. Specifically, "Every time you entertain pure thoughts and feelings, every time you decide to work for a high ideal, you are already in the new heaven, and this new heaven necessarily brings the new earth with it. For he who embraces a sublime philosophy is obliged to change his behavior and his way of doing things. All the methods that you are learning here with regard to nutrition, breathing, words and gestures... all this is the new earth."

Each creative pure thought and service, whether loving-light is beamed to angels of air, loving water while bathing, or giving a cookie to a child; all contribute to environmental harmony, peace and our emerging kingdom of heaven on earth, the golden age.

References

Toward a Solar Civilization   Omraam Mikhael Aivanhov

A New Earth: Methods, Exercises, Formulas and Prayers
    Omraam Mikhael Aivanhov

Life and Work in an Initiatic School: Training for the
    Divine   Omraam Mikhael Aivanhov

Harmony   Omraam Mikhael Aivanhov

The Solution Is You! – An Activist's Guide   Laurie David

A New Dawn: Society and Politics in the Light of Initiatic
    Science   Omraam Mikhael Aivanhov

Light Is a Living Spirit   Omraam Mikhael Aivanhov

You Are Gods   Omraam Mikhael Aivanhov